About the Author

Tom Heimer is a native of Yonkers, N.Y. and was a student of Jerome Sala. He received his Bachelor of Music in performance at Queens College of the City University of New York where he studied with Leon Russianoff. He received his Master of Music in performance from the University of Regina (Saskatchewan, Canada) as a Teaching Assistant and Assistant Conductor.

Mr. Heimer was a Band Director for many years in Thompson, Manitoba, where his bands won national and international awards, and was often a clarinet clinician and soloist at the Northern Manitoba Band Festivals. He has been a faculty member at the Saskatchewan School of the Arts summer band camp at Fort San, Sask. and has been a soloist throughout Manitoba and Saskatchewan. Mr. Heimer was Co-Principal Clarinet of the Saint John and Area Orchestra (New Brunswick, Canada).

In New York, Mr. Heimer has played with such groups as the Yonkers Philharmonic, Westchester Pops Band, first clarinet with the White Plains Pops Band, Solo E Flat Clarinet with the Yonkers Concert Band, and with the Port City Concert Band in Halifax. He is currently Principal Clarinet with the Westchester Band in New York since 1998 and has been a guest conductor and often featured soloist with the band. He and his wife Elizabeth reside in Dartmouth, Nova Scotia.

Tom Heimer

THE MOST ADVANCED CLARINET BOOK

AUSTIN MACAULEY PUBLISHERS™

LONDON * CAMBRIDGE * NEW YORK * SHARJAH

A CIP catalogue record for this title is available from the British Library.

ISBN 9781788785402 (Paperback)
ISBN 9781788785426 (E-Book)

www.austinmacauley.com

First Published (2018)
Austin Macauley Publishers™ Ltd
25 Canada Square
Canary Wharf
London
E14 5LQ

Dedication

This book is dedicated to my high school private teacher, the late Jerome G. Sala, an icon of clarinet playing, teaching and conducting in the New York area.

And thanks to David Dunn, a fellow clarinetist, for his digital design, music engraving, and layout work.

The Most Advanced Clarinet Book

The Most Advanced Clarinet Book is a collection of exercises, explanations and philosophies. Most are the author's original ideas as a result of experimentation and a few are those of his teachers. They attack the structural deficiencies of the instrument and idiosyncrasies that are necessary to master in becoming an accomplished player.

Some drills are note for note from orchestral /solo works that happen to address specific technical problems. Practising alternate fingerings is always suggested, even in situations where they are not appropriate. The philosophy is that if they are used often enough they become "second nature" and part of your arsenal. Total familiarity with all possible "left/right" pinky fingerings encourages "even" playing on all passages. "L-L" and "R-R" slides are always suggested even when not needed. A "right-left" switch while sustaining a note is always something to practice, even when not necessary. Altissimo C# should always be played without the RH Eb key, even in fast runs. Throat Bb should be played with the right hand side key at all reasonable cost, unless smooth connection is compromised too much. Low B/top line F# played with the ring finger flute fingering has a better tone on some clarinets and improves flexibility of that finger. Play it that way even when it is obvious not to.

The clarinet hasn't changed all that much since it's invention in 1690 or so. Overcoming it's mechanical problems is mental and repetitional. Hopefully this book will help.

CONTENTS

LEFT-RIGHT FINGERINGS:

1. This develops even playing with both pinkys, particularly the left. Playing EFGAGFE (3) using the left pinky on F is more difficult than using the right pinky F – you are moving fingers from alternating hands. So begin with right hand E. This also may be played starting with both pinkys E then right pinky F, which is much easier. Try both and compare. Start as slowly as needed for evenness and increase speed, always keeping it even. Next, substitute F# for F same process. Note that in (6) Bb and B alternate, throwing in one more thought process. Always use one continuous slur.

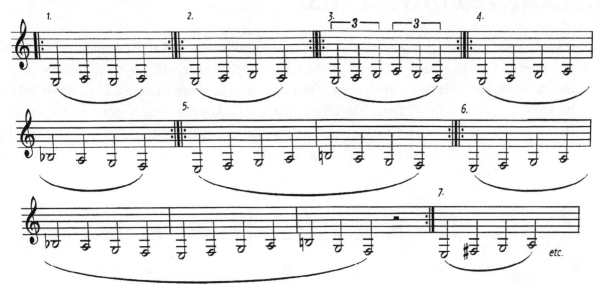

2. Tritones F to B. The purpose is to get used to playing these in tune, which should help with exercise 14 up an octave. These 2 exercises can be played one after the other. Vary the B fingerings and use one continuous slur.

3. The ultimate study in sliding R-R and switching L to R on the same note – even though you would never do this on these particular four notes.

4. This D minor arpeggio helps eliminate C from slipping in between the low A and D, requiring exact coordination of fingers from both hands. Play it first with the RH low F, then LH low F to make it harder (again, moving fingers of both hands at the same time). Also do this in F major and G major and minor starting on low G.

9

5.   More pinky coordination. You would never use both L+R on the same note unless switching pinkys, but do it here.

ALTERNATE FINGERINGS:

6.   Mixed major and minor triads. Finger coordination is mostly mental. Here all possible triads are covered. First use regular fingerings, then ALL possible alternates, even the ridiculous. Now mix them all while playing a triad. Start with lowest E as the bottom note and go up to 3rd line Bb as the lowest note of the triad. The high register would be the same fingerings. Stay even, start slowly, increase speed. Continuous slurring. You can switch the middle note (G,Bb,D,B, etc. then mix these two ideas (G,Bb,D,B,G,B,D,Bb).

7.   Practise on alt. F#/Gb. Vary speeds and mix the regular and alternate fingerings.

8.   High Bb exercise. G to forked Bb and back to G is difficult and not advisable, though some prefer it – good practise anyway. G to side Bb isn't all that easy either. Make the connections as smooth as possible – no "in between" notes.

9. Alternate Bb study. All Bs are flat in this exercise and should be played A key plus second from the top RH side trill key. This is one of the fullest sounding notes on the instrument as opposed to the normal throat Bb being the weakest. Not often used by many players, it can abused as it is difficult to connect to and from smoothly – particularly when going to a note using the RH (such as 3rd space C). Open G to alt. Bb is hard in itself. Connections to the Bbs must be smooth with continuous slurring.

10. This is for practise on F# to high D. Use the regular F# fingering first (this may be the one you use when sight reading). Next use the regular alternate F# and then RH 3rd finger flute fingering for index finger control. When playing slowly refer to exercise 23. Finally, mix up the fingerings and increase speed.

ALTISSIMO:

11. Don't use the RH high Eb pinky on the C#s. One continuous slur is best while repeating many times. Start as slowly as necessary to play it evenly and smoothly. The faster you can play it evenly and smoothly the better. This gets you used to playing the C# in tune without the Eb pinky even in fast runs.

12. A simple exercise to practise going to the altissimo and putting the RH Eb pinky down and up when appropriate. Play cleanly and build up speed. It may be played once or repeated many times with continuous slurring.

13. A continuation of previous exercise 12 but up to high G. Play it first with the regular high G fingering, repeating many times and building up speed. Then play it with G fingered thumb and register key only, a rarely used fingering that can be a little out of tune but provides for very smooth fast playing.

14. This is a progressive study on a very difficult interval. The objectives are to play in tune evenly with out any "slop" in between notes. Obviously this idea can apply to slurring down and up from any altissimo note to any lower one. F to B involves moving the left index finger for each switch as well as the RH Eb pinky. All F#s should be played by overblowing Bb (2 spaces above staff), as this is a rarely used fingering that is relatively in tune. Follow the fingerings exactly – note the use of RH C pinky instead of RH Eb pinky. This can at times be the more in tune choice. The final entry mixes them all up and should be played as sixteenth notes at quarter note=144. Always one continuous slur with many repeats.

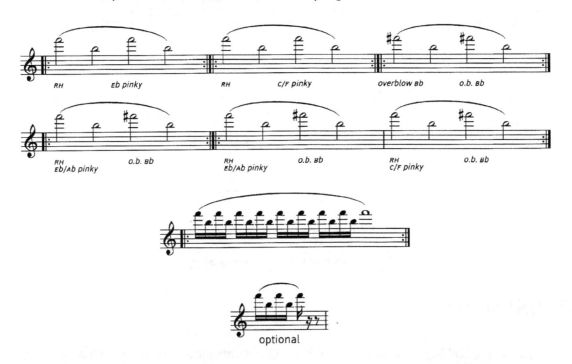

15. While this serves as practise for getting high A in tune, it is mainly for fingerings. Play the high E with the usual RH Eb pinky and same exact fingering for high A. Start with staccato or legato tonguing and progress to slurring, creating a lip slur on the last two notes. Next play high A with the RH C# pinky, causing the RH pinky to move, which is especially hard when slurring. You can slide the RH pinky or try just lifting it, still maintaining as smooth a slur as possible.

16. F-B tritones arpeggio. Follow suggested fingerings. First play the highest F covered with one repeat. Play it again with one repeat but now use the normal high F (RH Eb pinky) the first time and RH C pinky on the high F on the repeat. The RH C pinky is an underused fingering that often makes altissimo notes more in tune. High D is the only altissimo note it can't be used with, of course. Fingering middle line B with both L+R pinkys gives practise on not letting any Cs slide into the arpeggio. Start practising this slowly, then build speed. Finish by playing it slowly, then several times very fast and one more time slowly.

17. Altissimo practice. Purposes:
   - Going over the high break from B to C# thus having to move the LH index finger up and down while the RH fingers do the opposite. Smooth connection.
   - RH Eb pinky goes up & down to and from C#.
   - Even, in tune altissimo playing.

18. This is for intonation and smooth connections to and from high G. Play it first with the normal high G fingering then with the index finger of each hand (forked).

SPECIFIC STUDIES:

19. The Fulcrum. With the speed increasing, you have a finger exercise that covers many chords. After playing, now raise the Ab to A and lower the F# to F, leaving G always as the fulcrum. Keep raising and lowering those notes half steps until you reach octave skips. Try alternate fingerings, sliding pinkys etc. The widest skips are hardest. Try for the smoothest possible slurs. It can be started with any note as the fulcrum. Credit this to Leon Russianoff.

20. The "anything you want it to be" Fulcrum. Note the F# in the previous exercise is now an F. Continue to raise the second note a half step and lower the fourth note a half step. New skips are created.

21. Another Fulcrum variation. Same process. Obviously, you can make the second and fourth notes any notes you choose, but follow the half step up and down pattern. Eventually you should cover every possible skip.

22. Beat To Beat practising. This is for the difficult fast runs you encounter in your music, though you can also make up your own. It helps with fingerings and particularly with evenness. It's not really from one beat to the next, but rather from the start of each group of four (or three) to the first note of the next group. With group of four, also go to the third note of each group. Always start with the first notes of the run only, repeating (1) many times, then extend through the run to each stopping point, each segment with many repeats. When you reach the end (6). Now do the end part (7) many times by itself, you have practised this part the least. Credit this to Leon Russianoff.

23. G to high E slur. For a smooth connection slide the LH first finger slightly down and off the first hole slurring from G to E. No glissando or note bending. Slow practise is best. Going back from E to G put that same finger down very gently. Credit this method to Jerome Sala.

TONGUING:

24. The Tonguing Exercise. This is the first one of two to practise. It uses the clarinet's five simplest notes. You get practise at the beginning tonguing the same note three (then 2, 4, and 5) times followed by a step in between to the next set of three (2,4,5). So in effect, at one point you are tonguing three different notes in a row (CDE, EFG) . Start slowly then take a faster speed. Increase the speed until you reach a point where you can no longer do it neatly. Then practise that speed hundreds of times until your tongue and fingers are in sinc. Now going to the next faster speed, you will find that you do it well sometimes but not always. Now do that speed hundreds of times. After mastering a very fast speed try playing CDEFG at that speed. You should be able to do this since you already can play CDE and EFG that fast. Next, do the whole C scale up and down, then two octaves, then in all keys. Always start this with three repeated notes, which produces a group of four (which is easiest) and always start in C major. Be patient, as I went from terrible tonguing to good tonguing in about three months.

14

Try saying "Ta" very fast or just moving your fingers fast. Each by itself is very easy. Credit this study to Leon Russianoff.

25.   Advanced Tonguing Exercise. Same idea. All keys, then tongue up and down the scale. Next use groups of 2, 4 and 5 repeated notes. Now go up and down one, then two octaves mixing up the repeated note groupings. Tongue near the tip of the read and never bite. When tonguing long passages remember to concentrate even more as you near the end as your tongue simply gets tired and tends to slow down.

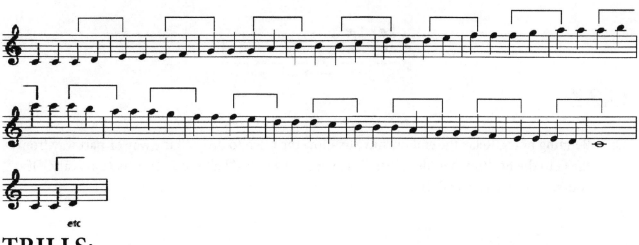

etc

TRILLS:

26.   Whole step trill. Start with your bottom note as low E and trill up a step to F#. Go up until your bottom note is throat Bb trilled to C above the break. Of course you want even trills, but the main purpose is to do them with all possible fingerings. For example, low B can be played middle finger, regular alternate (first finger plus key between second and third holes) and third finger flute fingering. For Eb use both regular fingerings plus all four forked fingerings even though they are out of tune (this also covers high register Bb). For first space F# use the alternate as well. On the last trill (Bb-C) play C first with the regular fingering for practise going over the break. See how fast and smooth you can do it. Then use the side trill key for C. Use regular throat Bb, then A plus the side trill key (second from the top). For low Ab-Bb do it with and without the RH Ab pinky held down. For the lowest note trill always do L-R and R-L. Vary it by also lifting pinkys when not necessary, striving to keep any low Gs from slipping in between.

27.   Half step trills. Same rules as the previous study. You may want to trill up from low E on whole steps and back down on half steps to cover everything. Another idea is to do it up and down

faster and faster one trill after another slurred, perhaps all trills on quarter notes, then on eighths, etc. Playing first space F-F# trilled with the regular F# fingering is an obvious challenge and also a situation that can occur (not a trill) during passages. The same can be said for low Bb-B.

28. A most difficult slur using the normal fingerings for both notes (no pinky for C#). Make sure your connections are clean and you play evenly. Increase speed to a trill, though you would normally use RH middle finger for the D# and probably not use a pinky when trilling these two.

JAZZ:

29. Bending notes. Relax the embouchure to allow the pitch to drop all the way or part way from the G to the F#. You may also partially cover the F# hole ("half hole" it). Situations vary. Of course it is much more difficult to do this using keys, but it can be done (B-C-B).

30. The glissando. Starting Gershwin's "Rhapsody in Blue" involves this B to C glissando, though the gliss. may start as low as low G. Uncover the holes gradually while adjusting your embouchure. You should have all fingers sliding off the holes at the same time with the lowest holes being vacated the most. Half way up your fingers should uncover as in the example – each finger off more than the next. Going over the break involves lots of embouchure change and very gradually lifting the pinkys to get over B and C. It is very difficult, but with maximum embouchure change is possible.

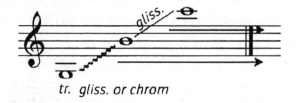

31. Glissando over to the altissimo. This example from the Artie Shaw Clarinet Concerto can be done several ways. The best way involves gradually covering the RH holes while uncovering the LH holes. Getting over from C to C# requires some embouchure change. The very difficult high G to high C is best attacked by glissing G to Bb with mostly embouchure change and then using

16

mostly gradual finger-lifting from Bb to C. It is possible to glissando from any note up or down to any other note, though some are of course much harder than others.

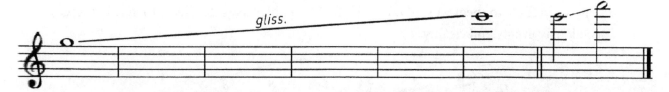

FROM ORCHESTRAL AND SOLO WORKS:

32.   From Ravel's "Le Tombeau de Couperin". A harder than it looks finger exercise. On the first six notes build for speed, make sure that the Eb side key is connected smoothly and cleanly, repeating many times with continuous slurring. Play the next part first without the added grace notes and using all LH pinkys on Cs and Fs. Next, add the grace notes with the second one played open G(*). Then play that G with the thumb plus Ab side key alternate, still using LH pinkys on all Cs and Fs. Finally, play it with all RH pinky Cs and Fs without the grace notes and repeat many times as fast as you can.

33.   A study on Tchaikovsky's "Nutcracker Suite" solo and on a grace note to E. Repeat each grace note fingering example many times then use each to begin the solo. Mix up the normal and alternate F# fingerings. The low E at the end can be used as the starting note for exercise 34 to combine the two.

34.   Finger exercise on the Stanford Clarinet Concerto. Follow the L,R pinky fingerings and alternate low B. Build for speed, then play it all with the normal fingerings even faster. For the top notes refer to exercise 12.

FINGERING EXERCISES:

35. This is a prelude to the next study. For the first two notes use L,R pinkys then R,L. Increase speed, play evenly and cleanly.

36. Though it looks easy, this is one of the most difficult exercises. The main problem is the F#, as the middle finger is the most difficult to coordinate evenly in a fast passage. F# to D means covering the two holes around the F# at the same time cleanly. Play the last C# first with the easier RH pinky then with the harder LH pinky. Next, play the first F# with the third finger flute fingering to exercise the least flexible ring finger. Start them all very slowly and increase speed only when it can be done evenly.

37. Playing the last five notes evenly after the first four chromatic ones is harder than it looks. Use alt. F#. These last five notes involve finger movements in alternating hands. The last three notes are surprisingly difficult to get perfectly clean when using RH side key for the A#. Repeat any groupings of notes separately or use "Beat to Beat" practising (exercise 22).

38. Make up random arpeggios. You find yourself without music, so make up an odd arpeggio and go back down on the same notes. Countless possibilities. Slur, tongue, any speed, tonal, atonal, whatever.

39. Regular and alternate Gb/F#. Play both G flats in each bar with the regular fingering. Next, play them both with the alternate (thumb plus LH side Ab/G# key) and last, mix them up. The highest note in the exercise can be any note, high or low.

40. This sequence of notes occurs quite often in clarinet parts. One must always decide between he regular or alternate B/F# thinking "Which is the lesser of two evils?" Use the regular fingering first, then the alternate and then the third hole flute fingering for good measure. Repeat each many times, then mix them up and increase speed with continuous slurring.

41. In this interesting staccato exercise each note should be played as short as possible. The group of seven need not be in one beat, just quite faster than the eighth notes.

42. A combination study in D major. Purposes:

- Short staccato, rhythmically exact.
- Going smoothly over the altissimo break, especially to and from high C#.
- Even, clean playing when middle finger F# is in the chord.
- L,R pinky work and alternating hand movements.
- For the mordent B-C#-B in the last bar use both the LH first finger alt. and thumb plus two RH bottom side trill keys alt. for the C#.

43. This is for practise going smoothly from the upper register to the altissimo. Best to practise it slowly but also play it fast. Connect smoothly from C# to E with the RH Eb pinky up for C# and down for E. Also use the RH ring finger on the F# for another variation.

19

44. The Left Arm Shake. This is not really a finger exercise, but a way to achieve an extremely fast (and more even) trill in a certain few cases. For these examples you can grip the right hand tightly and shake your entire left arm rather than just moving the LH pinky. You may even want to anchor the clarinet to your right thigh as well. There are a couple of other situations involving LH throat tones with the RH down (or not) and even one or two RH throat trills where you can shake the right arm. Experiment.

45. This run flows very easily. Use the alt. Bs and F#s(*) and RH pinky for third space C. Beat to Beat practising may help for evenness. Play it two times with continuous slurring as fast as possible. As long as it's even, speed is the only objective here. The last low A can serve as a first note of exercise 41 to combine the two.

46. Two simple exercises for when you are without music. Vary the articulations and mix them within the same scale. Do them on all major scales beginning on lowest E and ending on first line Eb major. Next do then on all the harmonic minor scales and lastly on the natural minor scales. Play evenly and the faster the better.

47. Variations on the previous exercise. Vary articulations as well.

48. More variations using whole tone scales.

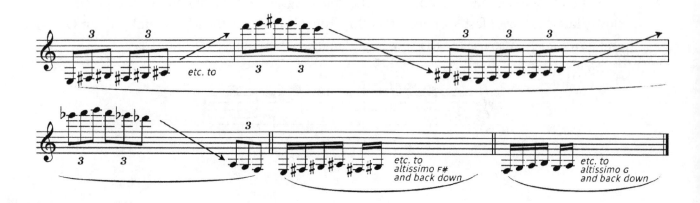

20

49.   This is an exercise for forked 2 (RH middle finger) Bb, alt. F#, pinky practise and extreme speed. Gradually increase the speed of the runs after the first Ab of this cadenza.

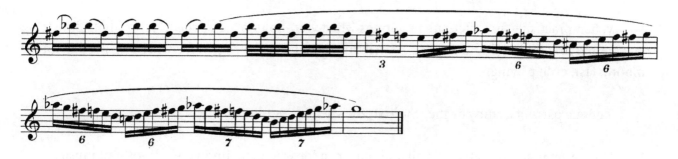

50.   Looks easy. Middle finger B is tricky Play it all slurred and lightning fast.

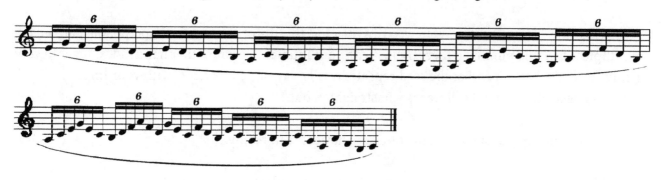

GENERAL TIPS:

Buy all the advanced method books you can find – tonal, atonal, scales, whatever. Also buy flute books as they include the very highest notes and a lot of octave skips, which are more difficult on clarinet than on the other woodwinds. Trumpet books contain lip slurs and special tonguing exercises. You can single tongue what they double and triple tongue.

Most of the time it's best not to try to play an exercise perfectly top to bottom. Just make sure you can play each passage perfectly. Go through the study once and flip the page for the next day. When that exercise comes around again it will be in effect like sight reading. Some players have a fear of sight reading, plus we tend to run out of things to sight read. Vary tempos as well. Perfect the pieces you will perform. I have never experienced "over-practising" a piece I intend to perform.

Accumulate two piles of books and alternate practising them each month. If you play Eb or bass clarinet mix them in with your Bb, A or C clarinets and practise a different one monthly so you get used to all of them.

When actually sight reading a study the first time really concentrate. You only sight read something once.

Write in the R,L fingerings on some exercises and not on others.

Use all the alternate fingerings randomly when playing a study. Then try it with the regular fingerings and alternates you would normally use. See how fast you can now play it. Play an entire study using the LH pinky on all low Fs and third space Cs as it is more difficult to coordinate movement between hands. Most of us learned the RH pinky F/C first and normally use it when possible.

When practising, use alternate fingerings when you shouldn't. Use the RH third hole flute (ring finger) fingering for low B and top line F#. All fingers must be developed for when you need them for smooth, fast, even playing.

Tongue parts of a study or the whole study when it's not indicated.

Have a set practise routine of half an hour or so for when you find yourself without music.

Buy a student model non-wood clarinet for travel so you don't worry about heat or cold.

Take the "warps" out of your reed by placing the tip of the wet reed perpendicular on the mouthpiece face and pinning it there tightly with your thumb. Use your other hand index finger to very gently "tick" the bottom end of the reed repeatedly (like saying "come here" with your finger). Repeat as needed. Eventually all warps will straighten out.

Add some jazz passages to your routine. They come in handy.

Musicality and intonation allow us to enjoy music. Lack of technique makes these two impossible. We play a mechanical monster.

INTRODUCTION TO THE FULL STUDIES:

The following etudes incorporate many of the 50 Areas of Study. The notes and articulations must be played as is (unless you feel like tonguing everything!), but the tempos, dynamics and interpretations are up to you.

Tom Heimer with the Westchester Band
Alan Hollander, Conductor
Chase Park, Scarsdale, New York

Slur, Fingerings

Speed

Scales and Arpeggios

Ascending Patterns

Increase speed. slur all "connected" notes, then vary articulations

Descending Patterns

Increase speed. slur all "connected" notes, then vary articulations

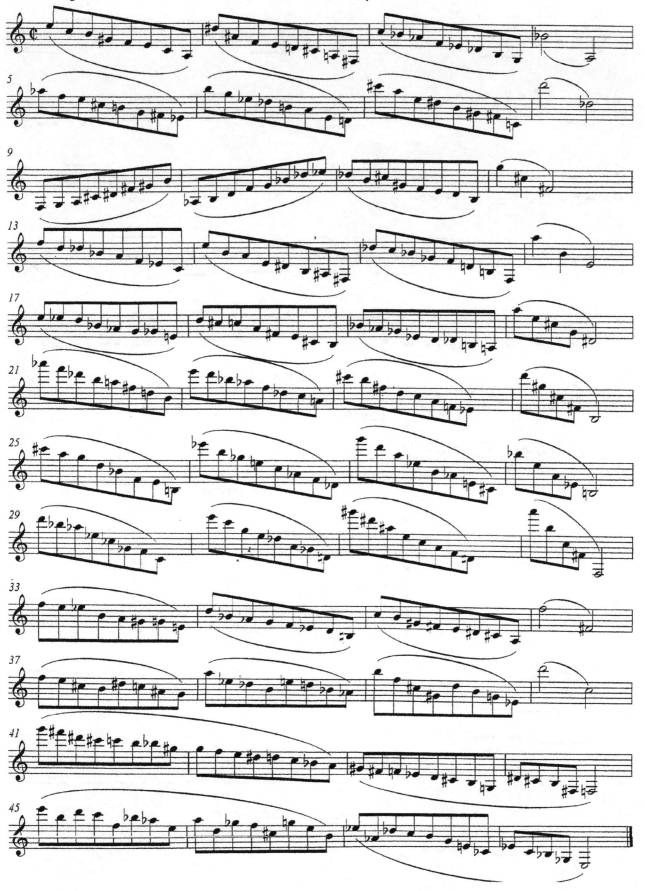

Articulation (Staccato or Legato Tonguing)

Tonguing

Same Note Staccato

Rhythm

Dotted Rhythms

Study in 7/8

Tarantella

Seconds and Thirds

Accidentals good throughout measure

Fourths and Fifths

Octaves and Sevenths

Small Skips

Skips

Accidentals good for one note only.

Mixed Accidentals

Mixed Time Signatures

Key Changes

Double Sharps and Double Flats

Trills, Shakes and Grace Notes

Glissandos, Note Bending, Trills

Mixed Tonalitites Free Flow

Ad lib: Rhythms are suggestions with no set meter or tempo. Whole tone, 12 tone, modal, pentatonic, accidentals for one note only.

The Roller Coaster

Cadenzamania

Tempos are suggestions, bar lines for accidentals only

48

The Most Advanced Study

From all 50 short studies.

CPSIA information can be obtained
at www.ICGtesting.com
Printed in the USA
BVHW012118160220
572479BV00031B/435